Just about a year ago I had the pleasure of taking my very first sprinting class taught by the incomparable, Ms. Nelson. She told us not to fret over the smallest of editing mistakes, and to write straight through with determination and abandon. So, I did. Before I participated in the first 10 minute sprinting session I was typing 21 words a minute. At the end of that session I had typed 439 words of the first chapter of my WIP, at the time. I have been sprinting ever since. Take this Guide as gospel. Follow the directions to the letter, and you will have success in every aspect of your writing. Because it works, folks. It's as simple as that.

Shannon Orso
Author of Sci-Fi

The

Sprinter's Companion

V.S. Nelson

SPRINTING

The Secret to Finishing Your Manuscript

Ever wonder why some authors are able to write four, five or six full length novels in a year? Surely, most of them can't afford a roomful of ghost writers who have managed to capture the author's real voice. Do they have some magical secret you haven't been privy too?

Ever find yourself sitting at the computer all day long only to discover your entire word count for eight hours was four hundred?

I know just how you feel. The old saying, *been there, done that* previously applied to this writer, but not anymore.

Too many times a writer will sit down at their computer and wait for those magical words to spontaneously appear. Or perhaps they are pondering over every word and rewriting every sentence before moving on. No wonder their work-in-progress is never completed.

If you are looking for a way to increase your daily productivity, and at the same time increase your word count then maybe you should give sprinting a try.

I'm often asked, how do I manage to constantly produce 5-10 thousand words a day? Do I live and sleep at the computer?

Of course not, no one can. I will admit I am a fast typist and I have a regiment I follow religiously, but that isn't where my secret lies. I'll try to explain in the pages that follow.

Back when I first started writing non-fiction, I took a lecture developed for college bound students and adjusted it for my personal use. That lecture was on *Time Management*, and utilizing it has saved me a lot of frustration. And even though they can go hand-in-hand, this session isn't on time management, it's on sprinting. My primary focus is to get you, the writer, to increase your daily word count. So let's get started, shall we?

Commonly Asked Questions

What is Sprinting?

Simply put, it's a simple method which will help you finish your novel's rough draft. The method utilizes small periods of time throughout your day which will enable you to produce more work and/or words per minute than merely sitting at the computer for endless hours. The end result will astound you. Not only will you be able to significantly increase your word count, you'll be amazed at the amount of household chores you can accomplish the same time.

Really? How is that possible?

I'll show you in the upcoming pages. Remember to pay close attention to the instructions. After a few rounds of sprinting you'll know what I'm talking about. Just be patient.

What about edits and rewrites?

Using the methods shared in the pages that follow, you will be able to sprint through rewrites and edits in record time. I've included a section for sprinting rewrites and edits in this manual.

I've been working on this manuscript for three years. Will I *ever* get this book written and ready to submit to a publisher?

Boy, does that sound familiar. I've lost count of the authors I've known that have spent two or more years on their manuscript. It's fantastic to have that much time on your hands to work on the same book. But what happens when you land a contract for more books? Surely the publisher isn't going to sit by and let you have a year or more to play with two or more books. Just recently a friend of mine landed her first contract. She spent over five years perfecting the first book. The publisher wanted two more in less than one year. Ouch! Needless to say, she was in a panic.

But guess what, after taking my sprinting class, the author has successfully met her deadlines and turned in two more full size edited books to the publisher in just a few months.

On a more personal level, I want the ideas out of my head and on to paper (or stored in the computer) so I can move on to my next story. I've got enough stories inside me to fill a small library just waiting to get out. Getting them on paper (or stored on my hard drive) is the first step in success. One of my favor sayings is, "you can't fix what isn't written." So worry about getting that rough draft out of your head and on to paper. I'll show you how to sprint through rewrites and edits later in this pamphlet.

How long are your sprinting periods?

You can adjust your sprinting times from 15-30 minutes. Small amounts of productive-precious time add up quickly as does your daily word count. You will be amazed what you can accomplish using the sprinting method.

I don't type very fast. In fact, I tend to henpeck most of the time. Can I use your method of sprinting?

Not a problem. Sprinting will work for everyone. Many of the authors I know still write in long hand. If they can do it, so can you. All that is required is your dedication to finishing your work-in-progress.

I am a planner and write from my outline. Will sprinting help me?

Of course it will. There is a sprint section specifically for you in this text.

Typing Speed

Before I ask you if you know what your typing speed is, I want you to know, your typing speed has very little to do with your sprinting speed or the amount of words you are actually able to put down on paper in any given time. The reason for that is typing speeds are based on copying someone else's work. It has little to do with the creating process, which is what most author's do when they sit down to write a novel.

Typing speeds are still used and asked for when you apply for a secretarial position. This allows the employer to guess at the amount of work you'll be able to produce for them.

Still, it can be useful to know your typing speed, so I've including instructions on how to find it. You can compare your typing and sprinting speeds later if you choose.

Do you know your typing speed?
If you don't know- here's a simple way to find out.

Open a large print book. Set it next to your computer where you can see it comfortably. Now set your timer for 5 minutes and type. Don't edit yourself, just type. When the timer goes off—stop. We are now going to figure out how many words you've written. A simple way, if you're in Microsoft Word, is to click on your Tools button, then on Word Count. Take that number and divide it by five. Presto, you have a rough estimate of what you can type in one minute.

Words produced divided by 5 equals your average typing speed.

Sadly, you're not going to be able to create a new story and hammer out *that* many words in a minute, but you can come pretty close if you follow my instructions.

Sprinting Speed

Let's establish what your sprinting speed should be.

Use this formula only if you already know your typing speed.

Take the number of words you normally type per minute.

Let's say your last typing test was 50 WPM.

Realize that you won't be reading from a sheet of paper nor will you have a Dictaphone plugged in.

You are creating a new work of art. You can't really **think of and create something new and still type 50 words per minute no matter what you do.**

So take your WPM typing speed and divide it in half. This should give you an idea of your average sprinting speed if you follow my directions…BIG if, I know, but this is how I keep my word count up and something to aim for.

Typing speed divided by two equals your ideal sprinting speed.

Don't worry if you don't achieve this number immediately.

The Basic Rules to Sprinting

Before we Begin there are a few rules you should follow.
This can be extremely hard for some, especially for those individuals who like to edit as they go, so it may take you a few sprints before you are comfortable with this system of sprinting.

Rule #1. DO NOT SIT DOWN, OPEN UP A BLANK SCREEN AND STARE AT IT expecting something to transpire. That's not going to happen, and it's one of the worst things you can do to yourself.

Rule #2. Unless you are sprinting in a group, make sure you're alone and going to be alone for some time. Constant interruptions will cause you to lose focus. I prefer total silence when I sprint alone. If you use music to inspire you, then by all means, turn on the stereo... but, not the television. Turn the ringer on your phone off and ignore incoming texts.

Rule #3. Get yourself situated with coffee, smokes, drinks or whatever makes you comfortable. Most importantly, have a kitchen timer or a timer on your cell phone or computer set up and ready to go.

Rule #4. Do not, I repeat, **DO NOT** worry about grammar, punctuation, spelling or anything else. You are here to type. Once your 60k words are down and the story is on paper you can worry about revisions.
Yes, it will be rough—really rough, but it's down and you'll have something to work with. Remember one of my favorite sayings, "you can't correct or edit what isn't down on paper!"
We'll worry about editing and revising your manuscript later, once you have a completed first draft.

Simple Sprinting Instructions

Sit down at your computer. Turn it on and open up your text document.

NOW close your eyes and formulate the first scene or the chapter you are working on in your mind.

Yes, I'm putting you into a meditative state.

See the scene coming alive. Using your senses, mentally see the action play out before your closed eyes. Hear the sounds and the conversation taking place. Take in all of the surroundings, attitudes, atmosphere... I can even smell his cologne. Can you? Once you have everything in your mind, I want you to...

Get up and stretch! You heard me—get up and walk away. Go potty, pour yourself a cup of coffee. Do whatever, but take a short break before you begin, but remember to focus and keep that scene in your mind. Give yourself five minutes, keeping the scene in your head first and foremost.

When you are ready, return to your computer station and reseat yourself.

Set your timer for fifteen minutes and start typing, remembering all the rules from the previous page. No backspacing, no correcting. Type out the scene just as you pictured it. Remember, you will correct typos later, but not now!

If you lose your concentration or forget something, close your eyes, bring the scene back to the foremost part of your mind and resume typing.

When the timer goes off, **STOP!** Of course you can finish that sentence. But stop with the timer. Now check your word count. MS Word, MS Works, and almost all word processing programs will have a word count at the bottom of the page. If not, highlight the section you just completed and click on the word count icon. Write that number down.

Get up and stretch your legs. Hit the bathroom again, refill your coffee cup, put in a load of laundry or do whatever you need to do during your break. If you are sprinting with others, you may want to discuss your accomplishments or word count. I've known many who used this time to brain storm their next section/scene.

Everyone I know adapts their sprinting to their writing style. Meaning, if you write extremely long detailed scenes you might want to adjust your sprinting session to twenty, twenty five or thirty minutes. I tend to write in thirty minute sprints and take fifteen minute breaks.

After my first couple of sessions and I'm fully awake, I utilize my breaks by putting in a load of laundry, turning on the dishwasher or making the bed. Remember what I said in the beginning about time management? Utilizing your breaks will help you accomplish the smallest of tasks between your writing times. It also keeps the hubby happy and the kids fed. <Grin> Try not to stay seated to check your email or network. Part of this exercise is to move… you need to get out of that chair and stretch. Too many authors suffer from carpal tunnel syndrome, bad backs and other ailments. If you are writing on a laptop, try to position yourself like you would at a desk top. In simple terms, do not place your laptop on the coffee table and bend over to write.

Setting the timer for breaks is not necessary, but if you tend to lose track of time, you might want to for the first few sessions or at least until you get this method down to a fine art.

So your break is over... NOW WHAT?

Resume your seat. If you did not finish your scene, read over the final line or two of what you previously wrote. (Not the entire 400-700 words, just enough so you know where you left off.) Close your eyes and picture where your scene picks up. If you finished that scene or chapter, picture the next one. When you are ready, open your eyes, set your timer and begin again.

It's really that simple.

Repeat as many times during the day as needed or is allowed. I understand we all have other obligations and demands placed on our time, so your sprinting schedule may be as varied as the books on your shelves. Just remember to utilize what time you have.

Sprinting For the Planner

There is very little difference between the *planner* and the person who writes from the seat of their pants, especially when it comes to sprinting.
The key difference is the planner will need to have their outline or notes next to them near the computer. The writer will, of course, need to review the outline prior to picturing the scene in their mind. Everything else is pretty much the same.
The Planner will want to set their timer, just like the *pantser* (person who writes from the seat of their pants), and take the appropriate amount of breaks.
When they return from their break, they will, once again, review their outline or notes then pick up where they left off after setting their timer.
All other rules and practices apply to both planners and pantsers.

Calculating the Time It Will Take To Complete
Your First Draft

Calculating your actual sprinting time. Take the total words you wrote in any given sprinting section and divide that number by the number of sprinting minutes.

Let's say you typed 420 words during your first fifteen minute sprint. Divide 420 by 15. You averaged 28 words per minute during that particular sprint. *Not too bad for a first timer.*
If you want to know your daily average, do this for all sprint sessions. Now add the total word counts for your sprint sessions and divide that number by the total number of minutes in your sprint sessions.
Example:
Session 1 – 420   1604 divided by 60min = 26.73
Session 2 – 390
Session 3 – 444   You averaged 26 minutes for all 4 sessions
Session 4 - 350
          1604 total words during your 4 sprints

So, how long will it take you to type out a 60K word novel?

That, of course, will depend on your dedication, your typing/sprinting speed, your sprinting time (15 to 30 minute sessions) and how many sprints per day you do.

Let's say you do four thirty minute sprints per day at 25 WPM actual sprinting speed.
That works out to 750 words for each 30 minute sprinting session or 3000 words per day.
At this rate it will take you 80–thirty minute sessions to complete a 60K word novel.

To figure this out on your own…

Take the 60,000 words needed and divide it by your daily average. The following model, I used 3,000 words per day as the average.
60,000/3000=20

Guess what? Your rough draft should be completed in 20 days!

SPRINTING SPEED BASED UPON SPRINTING SPEED

WPM	1- 30 Minute SPRINT	X 2 SPRINTS	X 3 SPRINTS	X 4 SPRINTS
10	300	600	900	1200
15	450	900	1350	1800
20	600	1200	1800	2400
25	750	1500	2250	3000
30	900	1800	2700	3600
35	1050	2100	3150	4200
40	1200	2400	3600	4800
45	1350	2700	4050	5400
50	1500	3000	4500	6000
55	1650	3300	4950	6600
60	1800	3600	5400	7200

I've included a section in the back of this pamphlet for you to record your actual sprinting sessions and word counts.

Say your editor has given you forty-five days to get that novel to him. You have taken twenty days to bang out a very rough draft. That leaves you twenty-five days to go back, re-read your story and make adjustments. Since I write full time, this is easy for me, but it may not be so easy for a working mom.

Revising and Editing Using the Sprinting Method

Once your rough draft is complete you will need to set aside editing time just like you did for your sprint sessions. You can work your edits similar to what you did during your initial rough-draft writing.

Sit down with the first chapter, set your timer and read through it aloud– yes, through all the mistakes.

You're bound to see several, but you're reading for FLOW this first time through. Ignore the mistakes! Yes, I said ignore the typos, etc—they will be fixed soon enough—I promise you.

By the way, this is the part that drives the grammar police crazy. Don't deny it, if are one. Just grit your teeth and bear with me.

Once you've read through the first section, ask yourself; is the flow right? Did I capture the essence of the scene?

Good. If not, go back and highlight those areas.

When the timer goes off, take a quick break and do whatever it is you want or need to do—smoke, drink, potty, laundry, dishes, etc. Come back when you're ready, or when your break timer goes off. I didn't mention this before, but many set the timer for their break periods. This helps keep you on tract. It's very easy to get caught up doing the *what-evers* and forget to return to your seat at the computer.

Now that you're back in your seat, set your timer and re-read that chapter again. Yes, again. This time you're looking for typos and misspelled words. Go ahead and correct them.

A normal chapter or scene takes me three sprinting sessions to correct. It may take you more or less, depending on the number of mistakes you've made while creating your rough draft.

Chances are the more you sprint the cleaner the rough draft will be and the more words you will type per sprinting session.

Practice makes perfect.

When I first started sprinting, my typing was barely readable. I was trying to put as many words on paper as I could in the given fifteen minute sprint session. If you find you are concentrating more on the word count then on accuracy, try slowing down just a bit. (Not too much, just one or two words per minute is all) It will save you time in the long run. I gave up the racer mentality and found a rhythm which works for me. Today, I'm happy to say, my typos are kept to a minimum and I have less work to do when it comes time for revisions and edits.

Remember to take your breaks—this is important for you, your eyes and your body.

When you're ready, go to the next chapter and repeat the process. When I do this, it usually takes me a few days, so allow yourself enough sprints to get through your novel with time left over.

Once you think you are finished, **TAKE A DAY OFF,** you've earned it!

The following day sit down at your computer with fresh eyes, go back and re-read your manuscript. You'll probably find sections that need tweaking or correcting. Make those small minor changes, but don't get bogged down with tiny little details. We all know we can edit something to death and still not get it right.
The original idea was to get something written and clean enough to send to your editor for approval, and this you will have. The editor will have ideas for the story and ask you to make more revisions. Worry about them once you hear back from your editor.

So there you have it, my method for constantly producing 5-10k words per day. I hope you'll give this simple method of writing a try and I hope it works for you.

Suggestion: Try different sprinting times to see what works best for you. I started out doing fifteen minute sessions, but soon discovered I was having trouble completing an entire scene. I adjusted the sprint time to twenty minutes, then thirty. Most of the time, depending on what series I'm working on, I sprint using thirty minute sessions. I take fifteen minute breaks which frees me up to start other projects, i.e., laundry, dishes, networking, checking my email, etc.

Try a few days using fifteen minute sessions, then a few days at twenty then thirty.

Find what works best for you keeping scene completion as your primary goal. I do suggest NOT setting your sprint sessions over thirty minutes. The strain on your back and other body parts is too much for anyone. If I didn't mention it before, writers can and do develop serious injuries from sitting at the computer all day long. These breaks help you in more ways than one. If you haven't already figured it out, that is one of the primary reasons I instructed you to get up, stretch and move during your breaks.

I've added a few pages to the back of this pamphlet as a sprinting journal with hopes you will use them to record your sprinting sessions.

Good Luck and Happy Sprinting,

Always, V

My Sprinting Journal - Day 1

Session 1   Minutes: _____

Word count: _____ **/ mins. =** _____   **avg. words
this session**

Scene: _____

Session 2   Minutes: _____

Word count: _____ **/ mins. =** _____   **avg. words
this session**

Scene: _____

Session 3   Minutes: _____

Word count: _____ **/ mins. =** _____   **avg. words
this session**

Scene: _____

Session 4   Minutes: _____

Word count: _____ **/ mins. =** _____   **avg. words
this session**

Scene: _____

Total words for 4 sessions _____

Total minutes: _____

Average sprinting speed: _____

My Sprinting Journal - Day 2

Session 1   Minutes: _____

Word count: _____ **/ mins. =** _____   **avg. words
this session**

Scene: _____

Session 2   Minutes: _____

Word count: _____ **/ mins. =** _____   **avg. words
this session**

Scene: _____

Session 3   Minutes: _____

Word count: _____ **/ mins. =** _____   **avg. words
this session**

Scene: _____

Session 4   Minutes: _____

Word count: _____ **/ mins. =** _____   **avg. words
this session**

Scene: _____

Total words for 4 sessions _____

Total minutes: _____

Average sprinting speed: _____

My Sprinting Journal - Day 3

Session 1   **Minutes:** _____

Word count: _____ **/ mins. =** _____   **avg. words**
                                                             this session
Scene: _____

Session 2   **Minutes:** _____

Word count: _____ **/ mins. =** _____   **avg. words**
                                                             this session
Scene: _____

Session 3   **Minutes:** _____

Word count: _____ **/ mins. =** _____   **avg. words**
                                                             this session
Scene: _____

Session 4   **Minutes:** _____

Word count: _____ **/ mins. =** _____   **avg. words**
                                                             this session
Scene: _____

Total words for 4 sessions _____

Total minutes: _____

Average sprinting speed: _____

My Sprinting Journal - Day 4

Session 1   Minutes: _____

Word count: _____ / mins. = _____   avg. words
                                                       this session
Scene: _____

Session 2   Minutes: _____

Word count: _____ / mins. = _____   avg. words
                                                       this session
Scene: _____

Session 3   Minutes: _____

Word count: _____ / mins. = _____   avg. words
                                                       this session
Scene: _____

Session 4   Minutes: _____

Word count: _____ / mins. = _____   avg. words
                                                       this session
Scene: _____

Total words for 4 sessions _____

Total minutes: _____

Average sprinting speed: _____

My Sprinting Journal - Day 5

Session 1   Minutes: _____

Word count: _____ **/ mins. =** _____   **avg. words
                                                                 this session**

Scene: _____

Session 2   Minutes: _____

Word count: _____ **/ mins. =** _____   **avg. words
                                                                 this session**

Scene: _____

Session 3   Minutes: _____

Word count: _____ **/ mins. =** _____   **avg. words
                                                                 this session**

Scene: _____

Session 4   Minutes: _____

Word count: _____ **/ mins. =** _____   **avg. words
                                                                 this session**

Scene: _____

Total words for 4 sessions _____

Total minutes: _____

Average sprinting speed: _____

My Sprinting Journal - Day 6

Session 1   **Minutes:** _____

Word count: _____ **/ mins. =** _____   **avg. words**
                                               this session
Scene: _____

Session 2   **Minutes:** _____

Word count: _____ **/ mins. =** _____   **avg. words**
                                               this session
Scene: _____

Session 3   **Minutes:** _____

Word count: _____ **/ mins. =** _____   **avg. words**
                                               this session
Scene: _____

Session 4   **Minutes:** _____

Word count: _____ **/ mins. =** _____   **avg. words**
                                               this session
Scene: _____

Total words for 4 sessions _____

Total minutes: _____

Average sprinting speed: _____

My Sprinting Journal - Day 7

Session 1   Minutes: _____

Word count: _____ **/ mins. =** _____   avg. words
                                                           this session
Scene: _____

Session 2   Minutes: _____

Word count: _____ **/ mins. =** _____   avg. words
                                                           this session
Scene: _____

Session 3   Minutes: _____

Word count: _____ **/ mins. =** _____   avg. words
                                                           this session
Scene: _____

Session 4   Minutes: _____

Word count: _____ **/ mins. =** _____   avg. words
                                                           this session
Scene: _____

Total words for 4 sessions _____

Total minutes: _____

Average sprinting speed: _____

My Sprinting Journal - Day 8

Session 1   Minutes: _____

Word count: _____ **/ mins. =** _____   **avg. words**
                                                     this session
Scene: _____

Session 2   Minutes: _____

Word count: _____ **/ mins. =** _____   **avg. words**
                                                     this session
Scene: _____

Session 3   Minutes: _____

Word count: _____ **/ mins. =** _____   **avg. words**
                                                     this session
Scene: _____

Session 4   Minutes: _____

Word count: _____ **/ mins. =** _____   **avg. words**
                                                     this session
Scene: _____

Total words for 4 sessions _____

Total minutes: _____

Average sprinting speed: _____

My Sprinting Journal - Day 9

Session 1   Minutes: _____

Word count: _____ / mins. = _____   avg. words
                                                      this session
Scene: _____

Session 2   Minutes: _____

Word count: _____ / mins. = _____   avg. words
                                                      this session
Scene: _____

Session 3   Minutes: _____

Word count: _____ / mins. = _____   avg. words
                                                      this session
Scene: _____

Session 4   Minutes: _____

Word count: _____ / mins. = _____   avg. words
                                                      this session
Scene: _____

Total words for 4 sessions _____

Total minutes: _____

Average sprinting speed: _____

My Sprinting Journal - Day 10

Session 1

Minutes: _____

Word count: _____ / mins. = _____   avg. words
                                                      this session

Scene: _____

Session 2

Minutes: _____

Word count: _____ / mins. = _____   avg. words
                                                      this session

Scene: _____

Session 3

Minutes: _____

Word count: _____ / mins. = _____   avg. words
                                                      this session

Scene: _____

Session 4

Minutes: _____

Word count: _____ / mins. = _____   avg. words
                                                      this session

Scene: _____

Total words for 4 sessions _____

Total minutes: _____

Average sprinting speed: _____

My Sprinting Journal - Day 11

Session 1   Minutes: _____

Word count: _____ **/ mins. =** _____   **avg. words
                                                             this session**
Scene: _____

Session 2   Minutes: _____

Word count: _____ **/ mins. =** _____   **avg. words
                                                             this session**
Scene: _____

Session 3   Minutes: _____

Word count: _____ **/ mins. =** _____   **avg. words
                                                             this session**
Scene: _____

Session 4   Minutes: _____

Word count: _____ **/ mins. =** _____   **avg. words
                                                             this session**
Scene: _____

Total words for 4 sessions _____

Total minutes: _____

Average sprinting speed: _____

My Sprinting Journal - Day 12

Session 1   **Minutes:** _____

Word count: _____ **/ mins. =** _____   **avg. words**
                                                                this session
Scene: _____

Session 2   **Minutes:** _____

Word count: _____ **/ mins. =** _____   **avg. words**
                                                                this session
Scene: _____

Session 3   **Minutes:** _____

Word count: _____ **/ mins. =** _____   **avg. words**
                                                                this session
Scene: _____

Session 4   **Minutes:** _____

Word count: _____ **/ mins. =** _____   **avg. words**
                                                                this session
Scene: _____

Total words for 4 sessions _____

Total minutes: _____

Average sprinting speed: _____

My Sprinting Journal - Day 13

Session 1   Minutes: _____

Word count: _____ **/ mins. =** _____   avg. words
this session

Scene: _____

Session 2   Minutes: _____

Word count: _____ **/ mins. =** _____   avg. words
this session

Scene: _____

Session 3   Minutes: _____

Word count: _____ **/ mins. =** _____   avg. words
this session

Scene: _____

Session 4   Minutes: _____

Word count: _____ **/ mins. =** _____   avg. words
this session

Scene: _____

Total words for 4 sessions _____

Total minutes: _____

Average sprinting speed: _____

My Sprinting Journal - Day 14

Session 1   **Minutes:** _____

Word count: _____ **/ mins. =** _____   **avg. words
                                                          this session**
Scene: _____

Session 2   **Minutes:** _____

Word count: _____ **/ mins. =** _____   **avg. words
                                                          this session**
Scene: _____

Session 3   **Minutes:** _____

Word count: _____ **/ mins. =** _____   **avg. words
                                                          this session**
Scene: _____

Session 4   **Minutes:** _____

Word count: _____ **/ mins. =** _____   **avg. words
                                                          this session**
Scene: _____

Total words for 4 sessions _____

Total minutes: _____

Average sprinting speed: _____

www.ingramcontent.com/pod-product-compliance
Lightning Source LLC
Chambersburg PA
CBHW072252310526
45795CB00011B/1040